Monster Motel

POEMS AND PAINTINGS BY
Douglas Florian

HARCOURT BRACE JOVANOVICH, PUBLISHERS

SAN DIEGO   NEW YORK   LONDON

Library of Congress Cataloging-in-Publication Data
Florian, Douglas.
Monster Motel/ poems and paintings by Douglas Florian. — 1st ed.
p.   cm.
Summary: A collection of poems introducing the monstrous dwellers
of the horribly horrid Monster Motel.
ISBN 0-15-255320-7
1. Monsters — Juvenile poetry.   2. Children's poetry, American.
[1. Monsters — Poetry. 2. American poetry.]   I. Title.
PS3556.L589M66   1993
811'.54 — dc20   92-7309
First edition
A B C D E

The illustrations in this book were done in pen-and-ink
and watercolor on vellum paper.
The display type was set in Lafayette and the text type was set
in Cheltenham by Thompson Type, San Diego, California.
Color separations by Bright Arts, Ltd., Singapore
Printed and bound by Tien Wah Press, Singapore
Production supervision by Warren Wallerstein and David Hough
Designed by Lisa Peters

For my brother,
Bill Florian

The Monster Motel

Welcome to the Monster Motel,
Where mostly monstrous monsters dwell.
They crawl the walls and gore the floors,
They shred the beds then saw the doors.
They box the clocks while chewing chairs
And throw each other down the stairs.
They beat the sheets then tear the towels,
They fill the night with hoots and howls.
They screech and scream and yip and yell
At the horribly horrid Monster Motel.

The Fabled Feerz

Have you seen the Fabled Feerz
With its fifty nifty ears?
Ears of green and ears of red,
Ears that walk across its head.

Ears tremendous, ears so small,
Ears that bounce a basketball.
Ears that jerk and ears that jiggle,
Ears that wave and ears that wiggle.

Ears quite fancy, ears most plain,
Ears that swing a ball and chain.
Ears with oil, ears with grease,
Ears that speak in Portuguese.

Ears shaped square and ears shaped round,
But something's strange that I have found:
For though the ears here do abound,
The Fabled Feerz hears not a sound.

Little Shy Shegs

Little Shy Shegs
Have two tiny legs
With two tiny toes
And that's all I knows
Of the little Shy Shegs
Since they never
Come out
Of their eggs.

The Monster Chef

The monster chef cooked up a meal
Of spotted toad and speckled eel.
He threw some socks into a pot
And boiled buttons piping hot.

He slowly simmered rubber hose
And steamed a lizard's pointed nose.
He griddled a fiddle and baked a rake
Then stuffed a statue in a cake.

He poached a roach and grilled a drill
Then smoked a broken windowsill.
He fried a frame and broiled a broom —
I think I'll stay inside my room.

The Gazzygoo

The Gazzygoo is green,
It grows grass on its back
And commonly is seen
Inside a sidewalk crack.

When Gazzygoos first meet
They go a little crazy:
They touch together feet
And grow a little daisy.

The Crim

The Crim cries a river
Of tears as it weeps.
It bawls by the barrel
And sobs as it sleeps.
It often looks gloomy
And always looks grim.
It's certainly lucky
It knows how to swim.

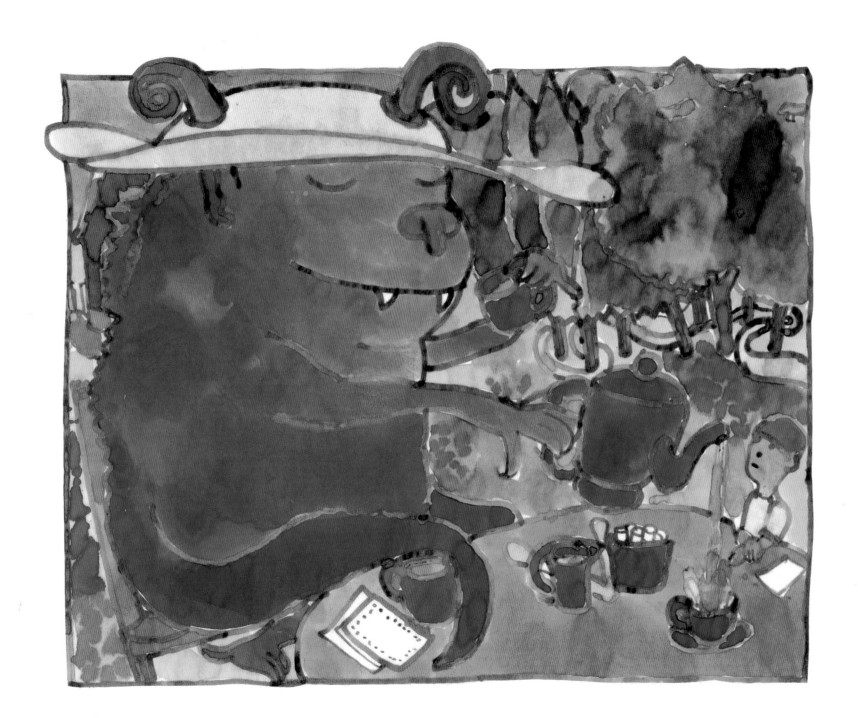

The Purple Po

The Purple Po is so polite,
With conduct most refined and right.
It shows the utmost courtesy
And manners whilst it's drinking tea.
At dinnertime it's never rude:
It doesn't belch or paw its food.
It has the grace and savoir faire
To help a lady with her chair.
I've never met a beast before
That's better bred to hold a door.
The Purple Po has so much poise
It hardly ever makes a noise.
It tips its hat and bows to greet you —
And then the Po politely eats you.

The Teek

The Teek is very tiny,
A short and stunted shrimp.
It's positively puny,
This peewee of a wimp.
It's very close to nothing
And very far from great.
Be careful not to step on —
    Oops, too late!

The Brilly

The Brilly is a silly beast;
It has no sense, to say the least.
It wears its shoes upon its hands
And ties its feet with rubber bands.

It climbs up on a tree branch high
To count the cows that float on by,
Then fishes in a mountain lake
For birds that swim there by mistake.

For lunch it munches traffic signs
And chews on unexploded mines.
Then sitting in the kitchen sink
It swallows quarts of crimson ink.

The Brilly is a funny fellow
Who takes its bath in lemon Jell-O
And goes to sleep beneath its bed
This foolish ghoulish puddinghead.

The Tweet

The Tweet has got a fleet of feet
With which it marches down the street.
Some feet are jumping up and down,
Some feet are heading into town.
Some feet are running to and fro,
Some feet have got no place to go.
Some feet are skipping to the right,
Some feet are hiding out of sight.
Some feet are learning how to dance,
Some feet are fleeing off to France.
Some feet are busy walking west,
Some feet think easing east is best.
A fleet of feet so very vast —
But Tweet is going nowhere fast.

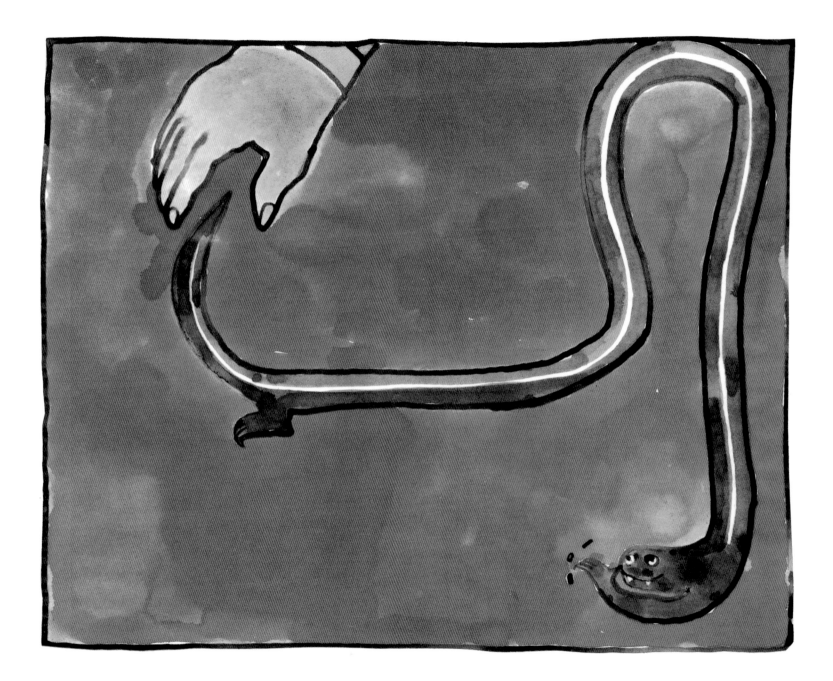

The Slender Slimy Slatch

The Slender Slimy Slatch
Is smooth and slick and hard to catch.
It slides and slithers on its side
And slips along its greasy hide.
A Slatch would make a lovely pet,
But no one's ever caught one yet.

The Beeky

The sneaky Beeky loves to hide
Both out-of-doors and home inside.
It changes colors on a chair
To match the pattern painted there.
And if it crawls onto a mat
It makes itself go very flat.
A Beeky on a chandelier
Can cast itself as crystal clear.
One sitting on the kitchen floor
Is very easy to ignore.
While clinging to a maple tree
It's near impossible to see,
And when it slinks across the street
It's most deceptive and discreet.
A Beeky's good at camouflage:
It disappears like a mirage.
So don't be mad if I disclose
A Beeky's hiding on your nose.

The Bleen

I am the Bleen
I'm very mean
I'm nasty and I'm cruel.
I steal, I lie,
I make you cry
I'm just a ghastly ghoul.
I've been a fiend
Since I was weaned
I'm selfish and I'm rotten.
Whatever good
I had in me
I've long ago forgotten.

A Monster's Day

Monsters creep and monsters crawl

Monsters bite and monsters brawl

Monsters steal and monsters snatch

Monsters hurt and monsters hatch

Monsters smack and monsters smash

Monsters tease and monsters trash

Monsters grab and monsters groan

Monsters mash and monsters moan

A monster's day is never through

With all those monstrous things to do.